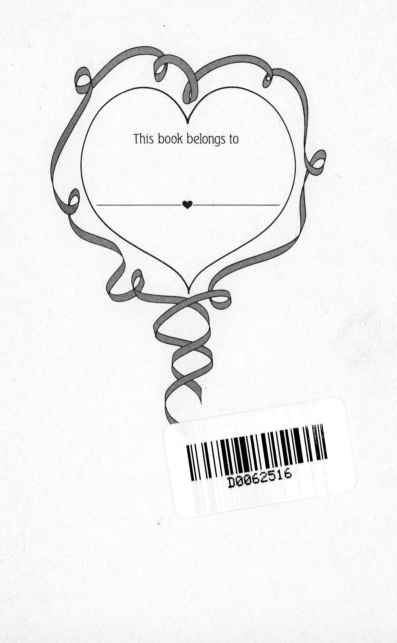

This book belongs to

— ♥ —

# Silent September

♥

## JOYCE
### LANDORF HEATHERLEY

**BALCONY PUBLISHING**

AUSTIN, TEXAS 78734

SILENT SEPTEMBER

Copyright ©1984 by Joyce V. Heatherley

**Library of Congress Cataloging in Publication Data**

Heatherley, Joyce Landorf
   Silent September.

   1. Consultation.    2. Suffering—Religious Aspects—
Christianity.    3. Heatherley, Joyce Landorf.    4. Temporomandibular
joint—Disease—Patience—United States—Bibliography.
I. Title    II. Series: Heatherley, Joyce Landorf.
BV4909.L26   1984       248.8'6       84–7490
ISBN 0–929488–01–6 (previously ISBN 0–8499–0377–7)

**Scripture quotations used in this book are from the following versions:**

The King James Version of the Bible (KJV).
   *The Living Bible* (TLB), copyright © 1971 by Tyndale House Publishers, Wheaton, IL.
   *The New Testament in Modern English* (Phillips), copyright © 1958, 1960, 1972 by
J.B. Phillips.
   *The Good News Bible*, the Bible in Today's English Version (TEV), copyright © American
Bible Society 1976.
   The New American Standard Bible (NASB), © The Lockman Foundation 1960, 1962,
1963, 1968, 1971, 1972, 1973, 1975, 1977.
   The Modern Language Bible (MLB), The New Berkeley Version in Modern English, Revised
Edition: Copyright 1945, 1959, © 1969 by the Zondervan Publishing House.

"Shortcut Home," © Copyright 1984 by Word Music (A Div. of Word, Inc.) All Rights
Reserved. International Copyright Secured. Used By Permission.

"Your Dear Face," © Copyright 1984 by Word Music (A Div. of Word, Inc.) All Rights
Reserved. International Copyright Secured. Used By Permission.

"I Cannot Wait," 1940, and "Too Tired to Feel," 1938, by Martha Snell Nicholson are
used by permission of Moody Press, Chicago, Illinois.

*Printed in the United States of America*

**First Printing, July 1988**
**Second Printing, June, 1989**

*Dear Joyce,*

*Pain is a language*
*without words—*
*and so it is untouched*
*by words.*

*Does it help to know*
*that my prayers*
*for you*
*are often wordless, too¿*

*And shaped like tears.*

—Susan Lenzkes

Pain has scraped away
the last visible traces of hope
off the edges of my soul.

♥

So begins my personal journal of pain, in the early months of 1982. It continues with,

Naively I always think that pain can do *nothing more* to me. Yet I am always wrong.

There is a certain amount of head knowledge within me that says someday the Lord, in His mercy, will step in and stop this hideous round of pain, which is attacking on a never-ending basis. Isn't that what a loving heavenly Father would do? Yet here, in my heart, I cannot see, hear, touch, or feel God; and the silence of my life is deadly. God seems to be doing nothing—nothing at all.

Continually I rationalize that after pain has robbed, raped, and smashed the courage and hope out of me, it will have spent its fury—like the last gusts of wind from a retreating thunderstorm. Often I fantasize that since pain has devoured so much of me already, my dues into the I've-suffered-enough-account have been paid in full, and there will be no need for further payment. Or, I think, at least pain will lessen the force of its rage and give me *some* respite from its devastation.

But, it seems I tend to underestimate the enormous penetrating power of pain. I minimize the tenacity of its excruciating grip. Somehow I hold tightly to the crumb of hope which says *maybe,* just maybe, I'll be mysteriously and miraculously given the grace and strength of God to go on, in spite of these crushing encounters.

Yet, with each new day pain swoops down like a huge demolition crane, swinging and smashing its steel and concrete ball of destruction against the flimsy walls of my battered body and soul. I'm left shattered, broken, and without a shred of hope.

I am no novice in walking the paths of pain. And I am no stranger to climbing the mountains of grief suffering. But this— this I do *not* understand, for suddenly I am aware that I don't hear the music anymore.

I'm a nightingale with broken wings. I'm a nightingale without a song. Oh yes, it's true that I'm a born "night-singer"—one who can sing the sweetest songs of God, even in the darkest dead of night. But now, now I don't hear the music of God or His angels; and I am frightened . . . alone . . . and hurting unbearably.

Someone told me today that they see a light at the end of my tunnel of pain. Someone else said I should rejoice in my "tunnel experience" for tunnels are the only way to get through the mountains to one's destination. And often, along our journey in this life, tunnels provide lessons and opportunities for growth. But, as another friend pointed out, there is a light at the end of my tunnel; however, it happens to be the headlight of a train which is coming straight at me, 100 miles an hour! The only lesson I'm learning here is that I'm going to be flattened like a pancake by this growing "opportunity." My soul panics at the scenario.

My life is consumed by my search for medical solutions, for

emotional enlightenment, and for theological explanations. But answers seem in very short supply. How many more mornings will I wake up hearing David's words, "This is the day the Lord hath made . . ." and then feel the icy grip of pain's reality remind me just what kind of a day it will really be?

I am also angry! And not just for me, but for millions of others. This is unfair. It's unjust. It's undeserved!

Is it conceivable that God stands passively by my bed of pain and says, "Of course I can heal you, Joyce, but I won't"? If this is true, then I am going to have a difficult time loving, trusting, or accepting this heavenly Father. It seems there is a theory that says God *can* heal me, but because I am doing something which blocks His will from being accomplished, He won't. This crushes all hope within me and God begins to sound remarkably like some earthly fathers I've observed. Fathers who could say, "I love you," but won't. Fathers who could affirm and encourage their children, but won't. This comparison between a heavenly Father and an earthly one becomes increasingly disturbing to me.

Or, does God sit on the edge of my bed when I am writhing in the highest level of pain—just before insanity—when I am crying out to be rescued and, at that fragile moment in time, calmly say, "My child, I want everybody well, including you, but Joyce, you're doing it all wrong. You need to read the instruction manual. You need to claim the right formula. You need only to follow the ten easy steps to healing"?

On the other hand, would the God I love and serve be chastising me by allowing this pain? Is He teaching me a lesson? What kind of a father punishes his child when the child is *not* disobedient? What kind of a father goes on teaching a painful lesson long after the child has *learned* it?

I don't know where to turn for help anymore. The darkness is too deep, and the God-silence is too great. I am isolated, lonely, untouchable. Worst of all, because I can't hear the music of God anymore, I feel like an abandoned orphan. Maybe someday someone will come along and rescue me, adopt me, and hold me in their arms of love until the pain subsides. But who? I've sung and written the music of God for thousands of others. Won't anyone now sing for me? Won't anyone bind up what pain has broken and help me hear the music once more? ♥

*Intolerant people
have never suffered.*

—Charles Swindoll


*Tolerant people
have been broken by suffering
one way or another.*

—Joyce Landorf

♥

Perhaps, to you, the words from my journal read as insignificant, mundane, or highly manufactured. If this is so, then I would guess that you personally have not experienced prolonged suffering; nor have you observed the destructive ways of pain at work in someone close to you.

I can understand your feelings and your frame of reference; for, should I have read these words ten years ago, I might have had your same thoughts.

However, to millions of people, including myself, chronic pain has become a most common, bewildering, and shattering way of life. And when I write or say things like,

The scissors of pain have cut all the chords of joy, humor, faith, and hope—and I am left dangling above a deep, black hole of despair . . . ,

people in all walks of life, of all ages, and of all races, or creeds, shake their heads in knowledgeable agreement. As one hurting woman wrote, "You have to really experience physical or emotional pain personally to be soul sisters in the special sorority of the suffering."

So I write these words to those of you who have not, up to this point in your life, experienced the annihilating damage that prolonged physical or emotional pain can produce. But I also write to others, like myself, who have paid our longtime dues into the "special sorority of suffering" and remain in that vast assemblage of humanity who are, as yet, unhealed.

I am not addressing the *causes* of our pain, for that's a vast, uncharted ocean, too complicated for my tiny, fragile boat. But rather, I write from the perspective of examining the *effects* of suffering, whether the actual cause originates from an emotional, mental, or physical source (or, in many cases, a combination of all three).

Because of the *effects* of suffering in my own life, I have a need to ask God questions, a need to define my own concept of God, a need to seek diligently for *God's* truth, and an aching need to be held and comforted by God Himself.

One of the most burning questions in my own heart is: How do we live with suffering? How can we apply James's message to a suffering Jewish community when he wrote, "Consider it complete joy, my brothers, when you become involved in all sorts of trials" (James 1:2, MLB)?

Or, as J.B. Phillips translated the same verse, "When all kinds of trials and temptations crowd into your lives, my brothers, don't resent them as intruders but welcome them as friends!"

*Friends?* How can we, day after day, welcome pain—and the acute suffering which accompanies it—as a friend? Pain, as I have experienced it, is not my friend, but my surest enemy. No longer is pain jabbing at me to "point the way" to something more serious. No, now it is my constant companion—relentless and ruthless as it ravages my body, mind, and spirit.

I know intellectually and theologically that the specific product produced by pain and suffering is endurance. James calls suffering the "proving of our faith," which brings out endurance, steadfastness, and patience. But how do we endure one more blow? One more day? Or, as my friend who had suffered several miscarriages said, after adoption plans for another child had fallen through, "It was another [one more] funeral." How do we go on?

I don't know how others are doing it, how others are making it through the night, or how others continue to sing and dance when they can no longer hear the music. But, here are some lessons from the classroom of my pain. The studies are tough—but I am enduring, I am continuing, and I am beginning to hear the music once again even though my circumstances of pain have not changed.

I want desperately to reach you and give you a cup of hope. I want to walk beside you as you exercise and strengthen the muscles of your endurance. But mostly, I want the words on the pages of this little book to hug you back to life and to convince you to stay one more day. ♥

## I CANNOT WAIT

I cannot wait to have Thy hand
  Wipe all my tears away
When I at last before Thee stand;
  Lord, dry them now, today!

I am so buffeted about,
  So worn and torn with pain,
My tortured flesh grown weary of
  This couch where I have lain.

I know, and yet my cup has grown
  Too bitter, Lord, of late.
Pour for me now some honeyed draft;
  It is so hard to wait.

I know that sometime I shall feel
  Thy touch upon my brow;
My heart will melt with love and joy,
  But Lord, I need Thee now!

—Martha Snell Nicholson

♥

*August 1982.* We were in Hawaii, on vacation with our children and grandchildren, when my jaw and head pain reached epidemic proportions. I slept in every morning, hoping to delay or change the patterns of pain—but it was to no avail.

One morning I got up and groped my way into the kitchen of our rented condo and found this letter from my daughter, Laurie.

Hi Mom,

I've been trying to keep James quiet all morning while I picked up things a bit. (Do you remember how *hard* it is to keep a two-year-old boy quiet? It's impossible!)

I've been thinking about you all morning. I don't understand your pain, but I love you so much, and I accept whatever you are feeling.

You are the one in your own private suffering. I am the one

watching. It is through the eyes of my love that I watch, love, and comfort you to the greatest ability of my heart.

You are precious to me. I don't want to lose you. (In the same way, if the tables were turned, you wouldn't want to lose me.) *But,* I don't want you to suffer any more. (You wouldn't want me to continue suffering, either.)

Loving someone is such a risky business—but, oh, I have been so richly blessed by my loving you. You are very special to me, Mom.

On your heavy pain days I sit in your balcony, cheering you on. And if the day comes that you *do* go home—I will feel a loss so great that it will be unbearable at times; however, a part of me will be relieved—for you will suffer *no more.*

My heart is with you.

Everybody, including James and I will be on the beach. The sun is finally shining. Come down and join us, when you feel like it. There is fresh cut papaya in the fridge . . . your favorite. Enjoy!

> See you later,
> Lovingly,
> Laurie

The poignancy of Laurie's note penetrated my heart. Yet, for all its sweetness, I could only taste the bitter sourness of my hideous pain.

I held her words in my hands for a long time, as if by holding the piece of notepaper I could absorb some of its comfort. But I couldn't. Eventually I went down to the beach to be with my husband and family. I tried making a stab at being as near-normal a Joyce as I could be. However the pain made it a useless exercise. So, as I studied the dear, bright faces of my family (especially my grandbabies), I mentally prayed prayers of blessing for each one, and silently spoke my final farewells. It was for me—as I know it must have been for my mother, when she was in the process of dying—a time to mourn my own passing. And I was quietly submerged in a deep pool of bereavement.

That day marked for me the end of a very long, tedious race— a toilsome race without a finishing line. I had no more strength and no extra reserve supply of energy to run and jump on the medical merry-go-round of alternatives. No longer could I go in search of new doctors or new and different specialists. No more could I bear another round of orthodox or unorthodox procedures. No way could I submit to more tests and X-rays. Nor could I bear another therapy session with a psychologist, counselor, or psychiatrist. The race had become a ride; and, like the race, the ride went nowhere.

So it was that in August, in the best and the worst year of my life, at fifty years of age—with beautiful children, good family and the incredible call of God upon my life—that I lost completely the will to go on.

Pain had destroyed my sense of humor, annihilated my ability to think logically, and had done its best to shatter my relationships with my husband and family. I simply did not care about one single person, thing, or event. I just wanted to be out and off this planet. I wanted, most of all, to go home to be with God.

Coming back to California after our vacation, I found there was yet another serious problem to work through.

Do you realize that if you are a Christian and unable to find a meaningful purpose for your life—having lost all hope, and longing to die—you cannot tell a single soul? If you do whisper the concept that you long to be with God, your inner self is exposed to the maximum level of your vulnerability. You become a sitting duck for a direct shot of instant rejection or harsh, critical judgments especially from the Christian community. I know this to be true because of firsthand experience.

Isn't it funny—no, make that *strange*—how, from almost the moment of our conversion (sometimes even from our parents), the computers of our minds are programmed with the *Pilgrim Progress* concept. That is, we are taught that we are pilgrims, just passing through this valley called life; and that the goal of our journey, and ultimate reason for our existence, is to personally experience the glory, the authentic peace and joy, that will be ours only when we go to heaven and see Jesus, face to face. But, here's the conflict. If I *say* I really want to go home to heaven, and I mean *right now,* it threatens the body of believers into a stunned silence, an instant sermon, or an icy put-down.

During this time, *with few exceptions,* I found that it was an extremely rare person to whom I could openly share my thoughts about going home to be with the Lord.

One exception was my friend—author Gloria Hawley. She phoned me one day when my pain was in level three and about to rise into level four (my highest level of pain endurance).

Gloria's understanding of pain and suffering of all kinds has come from her experience as the mother of two severely handicapped children who are now young adults. She is no stranger to the despair and depression which continually accompany pain.

Simply, she said, after hearing my despondency, "Don't you wish you could just go up to heaven, sit on God's lap, and take a nap for fifteen minutes?"

Oh, yes, Gloria! That's exactly what I would have loved to do!

Another person who understood what I was saying, even better than myself, was my close friend and publisher at Word Books, Francis Heatherley. He captured the essence of my desire and dilemma in a letter where he stated,

> . . . as difficult as it is for me to mention it, I must talk to you about one other thing that is continually on my mind and heart. This is, your desire to leave your pain behind.
>
> Please notice that I have expressed this desire of yours a little differently from the way you have come to state it. You say you want to go home. Please forgive me for arguing with you a bit, but I believe that what you want is not necessarily to die, but more likely that you want to be relieved of the agony of your body and a certain vacuum within your spirit. Tell me, if that pain were relieved and that vacuum filled, would you not fight for life 'til your last breath and toehold?

Good question! I faced the reality that I was not suicidal—as the world diagnoses suicidal—but, rather, I wanted desperately to be *out* of pain. Then, since heaven has no pain, no tears, and is the home of my heavenly Father, I wanted to be *there* instead of *here*.

From my early, tender years I was taught one of the strongest tenets of our faith: that heaven was our ultimate destination. For years I've sung the great hymns of the church which extol the glories of seeing Jesus face to face.

Even the apostle Paul voiced his preference for leaving this life and being with Christ. His letter to the Philippians said in the very first chapter, "For to me, living means opportunities for Christ, and dying—well, that's better yet!" (Phil. 1:21, TLB). So the desire and dilemma is an ancient one. How I love Paul for being unafraid to say, "Sometimes I want to live and at other times I don't, for I long to go and be with Christ" (Phil. 1:23, TLB). And he was being extremely realistic when he stated to the people of Corinth, "How weary we grow of our present bodies" (2 Cor. 5:2, TLB). Later, in that same chapter, he talked of dying when he wrote, "And we are not afraid, but quite content to die, for then we will be at home with the Lord" (2 Cor. 5:8, TLB).

Out of this world's pain and suffering, into my heavenly home? Sounds like a marvelous plan to me!

Be gentle and patient with those of us who, like Paul, have grown weary of our present bodies. For the suffering of this life—whether physical, emotional, or mental—forcefully pushes us heavenward like nothing else. ♥

## SHORTCUT HOME


Remember Lord, when I was so young,
So full of faith, and coy
The world all free from pain and doubt,
A kaleidoscope of joy!
But then there came that little pain
The one I hardly knew;
An ache, a knife, then silent screams
And now my life is through.

I know I shouldn't stop my days
Leave family and friends,
But something's snapped—the pain has won
So this must be the end.
I'm coming home to be with You
Or should I really try to stay¿
Could You have meaning in such pain¿
Oh God, I want to fly away!

*I'm coming home to be with You*
*There's nothing left for me to give,*
*Or can I live my pain, for You¿*
*Dear Lord, I'll try, I'll try to live!*
*So I guess I'll stay, just one more day,*
*And handle what time will bring.*
*I'll live my life and give again*
*But this one song I'll still sing—*

Chorus:

*I wanna come home and be with You, dear Jesus,*
*I wanna come home and see Your face.*
*I wanna come home and be with You, dear Jesus,*
*For I'm sick and tired of this lonely, painful place.*

*I'm sick of this place*
*and I'm tired of the race*
*and I can't stand the pace,*
*So I wanna come home*
*and be——with——You.*

—Keith Miller

♥

The month of August smoldered into a hot, California September. I came home from Hawaii neither rested, refreshed, nor eager to run the race, but tired, irritable, and with a new wave of pain.

As I look back on it now, I see that according to my calendar, I was immediately immersed in my usual high-stress level of activities. There were speaking engagements, family gatherings, writing schedules for *He Began with Eve,* a ton of yet unanswered mail, and a strangely silent God.

I discovered, however, that while God was silent at that time . . . His children were exactly the opposite! The phone rang constantly, and the mail was full of letters from Christians who were responding to my chronic pain problem.

Hundreds of those calls and letters were filled with loving, affirmative statements. I thanked God for every time I heard (or read) the words, "I love you Joyce . . . I wish I had some answers for you, but I don't . . . I'll lift you to God's throne daily, dear Joyce. . . ."

But many, many more letters—though sent by well-meaning, sincere Christians—were extremely destructive. Those letters had a crippling effect on my emotions and greatly damaged my overall spiritual well-being.

The general subject of each of those letters was usually why they felt I had not been healed, after nine years of pain from T.M.J. (temporomandibular joint stress dysfunction).

Some letters fairly screamed, "What's the matter with you . . . don't you believe Jesus can heal you?" However, the most often repeated phrase went—and still does, for I am still receiving these kinds of letters—like this, "I know *why* you are not healed." Then that would be followed by their own evaluation of my relationship with God.

Their spiritual diagnosis would read like a multiple-choice exam:

You are not healed because
  A. You do not have enough faith.
  B. You *obviously* have sin in your life.
  C. Both of the above.

One woman wrote, "Why don't you swallow your pride and your prejudice and go to [she named a TV faith healer] and get healed? He could heal you if you weren't so stubborn and filled with pride!"

At the same time I was dealing with these people and their judgmental attitudes about my spiritual health—and feeling the strong sting of their rejection—I had to deal with yet another problem. There was a drastic change occurring in my own personal prayer time with the Lord.

I was aware that hundreds of sensitive, caring Christians, in countless churches all over America, were praying for me. Everywhere I spoke, that whole year, the loving prayer support on my behalf was as incredibly good as the negative letters were incredibly bad. But, in my own life, I was shocked to find, I couldn't pray. Oh, I could pour my heart out to the Lord, as I always had. I could keep a running dialogue going with Him. But *only* if I was praying about someone else.

I'd tell God about some family disagreement or of a damaged relationship. I'd bring Him the hurts of people I'd met at my speaking engagements. Or, I'd petition Him about a friend's deep-heart-need. And I *knew* God was listening, and that He was with me. I'd sense His presence, hear His wisdom in His Word, and feel His touch in my mind and emotions.

But during that most uncommon September, while I found I could pray for others, I could not petition God for myself. It was amazing! If I began even a few words about my jaw or the particular level of pain that day, a ceiling would close between God and me. His presence, His joy, even His peace would vanish into thin air. Suddenly I'd be alone . . . talking to myself. Praying about myself was a ridiculous exercise in futility. It was as though my knees, stiffened by continuous pain and disappointment, would no longer bend in prayer.

Where did God go? And why did He go, for heaven's sake? What lesson was I supposed to be learning out of all this? Haven't we been promised that He would never, *never* leave us?

While I didn't know it then, I know it now. I'd just come face to face with a common obstacle God's children have encountered in their prayer lives over the centuries. It's that desperate moment in our lives when we are too sick, too crushed, and too tired to pray for ourselves.

My heart responded to the words I found in Martha Snell Nicholson's book *Wings and Sky* because she too was familiar with the obstacle found in praying.

> Too tired to feel, Lord,
> Too tired to pray,
> Words come so hard, Lord,
> What could I say?
>
> Too tired to feel, Lord,
> Aught but this pain.
> Through what long nights, Lord,
> Here I have lain!
>
> Sometime I'll work, Lord,
> Sometime I'll pray,
> Praise and adore Thee,
> But not today.
>
> Blessed assurance,
> He understands.

> Just let me rest, Lord,
> Safe in Thy hands.

Only unlike Martha, I couldn't find the "Blessed assurance" . . . it was *most* puzzling.

The silence of God was overwhelming. Not hearing Him or His music in my mind and soul was simply devastating. I was, as my special friend and author Keith Miller described, "Walking the rim of the world and hearing the crumbling noises beneath my feet."

It was the first week of my silent September, and the "crumbling noises" beneath my feet were deafening.

I wanted to die. ♥

> The thought of my pain,
>     my homelessness, is a bitter poison.
> I think of it constantly,
>     and my spirit is depressed.
>
> Lamentations 3:19, 20 (TEV)

*For the Lord will not abandon*
  *him forever.*
*Although God gives him grief,*
  *yet he will show compassion too,*
*According to the greatness of his*
  *lovingkindness.*
*For he does not enjoy afflicting men*
  *and causing sorrow.*

—Lamentations 3:31–33 (TLB)

♥

My pain had won. I felt there was nothing left inside me to give. My spirit was crushed and broken. Yet I wondered if I had the "right" to die. The more I thought about dying the more I realized I had to justify my thinking. Call it rationalization or whatever; I don't know, except that I sat myself down and methodically proceeded to make up my own "T" account. It was a simple list of pros and cons entitled, "Why keep on living?"

On the positive achievement side, the list was long and fairly impressive. I read:

- Married for thirty years.
- Gave birth to two children who started out and stayed marvelous.
- Thrilled with my role as mother-in-law.
- Fulfilled to be Grandma Joyce and Mama Joy to several beautiful grandbabies.
- Completed sixteen books in fifteen years.

- Recorded over a dozen speaking (cassette) tapes.
- Hosted my own radio program.
- Spoken all over the world.
- Made a film series of *His Stubborn Love*.
- Had a very special ministry and calling from God.

The con side of this list merely recorded:

- Nine years of jaw and head pain.

As I reread the "T" account, I felt that for my fifty years I'd been very blessed by God and had, with His strength, accomplished enough. I also felt I'd suffered enough. Now, I reasoned, it was time, because of the immense pressures of pain, to go home to my heavenly Father.

On the fifth day of that September, our daughter Laurie drove down from her home to see me. She was genuinely horrified at my lack of hope, my reasoning process, and my desperate desire to die.

"What do you want me to do for you, Mom?" she asked somberly. I looked at her for a second and then pleaded, "Release me, Laurie. Just release me so I can go."

I think she really understood that I was asking her permission to, in some way, take my own life. But all she could do was hold me, weep, and say over and over again, "I can't, Mom. I just can't let you go."

By the time Laurie returned home, the full force of the enormity of my circumstances and my fragile state of mind broke over her soul. Her heart was demolished. In her panic, she called our family's good friend and physician, Dr. Jitu Bhatt. Pouring out her fears, Laurie told Dr. Bhatt that they'd all lose me unless someone convinced me to stay. When the doctor asked her who I would listen to, Laurie answered, "Doc Heatherley at Word Publishing or Pastor Chuck Swindoll." Our doctor made his decision quickly. Since my friend at Word Publishing was in Waco, Texas, and my friend Chuck was in Fullerton, California—he'd call Chuck.

That very night I personally met with my dear friend Chuck Swindoll, a great and caring man. Many of you have come to love Chuck through his ministry as a church pastor, his radio programs, or his insightful books. But on the night of September ninth, I loved him because he'd cancelled his entire evening schedule to come to me in the greatest moment of my despair.

Since it was a hot, sultry evening in Southern California, and I felt oppressed inside the house, I suggested that we walk together.

As we approached the corner street lamp, Chuck's first words were, "You don't have *any* hope, do you?" And with that insightful observation he gave me the freedom to open up my heart. I knew I could be as vulnerable as I wished, so I began to lay out the extent of the hopelessness in my daily existence.

"I don't hear the music anymore, Chuck . . . and without the music of God, I can't go on.

"And," I continued, "what am I going to do with my feelings over all the letters that tell me I'm not healed because I've got sin in my life?"

Chuck's natural sense of humor surfaced for just a moment

and he said, "That's it! Joyce, if you just had a little *sin* problem, I could fix you up just like that!" He snapped his fingers. "We evangelical pastors are good at that. I'd tell you about repentance, forgiveness, and reconciliation!" We both laughed and then soberly he continued, "But you tell me you're holy before God, and you're suffering . . . without hope. And I don't *know* what to say or do. I just don't have big and glorious answers for you!"

"Then at least tell me," I pleaded, "what I'm going to do with verses such as 2 Corinthians 12:9, 'My grace is sufficient for thee' (KJV), when some days there seems to be no 'grace' at all. And what can I believe about Paul's words, when he wrote, 'I can do all things through Christ which strengtheneth me' (Phil. 4:13, KJV)—when I can't even write my name, much less books, when I'm in level four pain? But," I confided in Chuck, "my darkest fear is over a couple of verses my dear friend, Joann Letherer, gave me . . . they're in Acts, chapter 9, verses 15 and 16. They talk about Paul being *called* to suffer. What if the Lord's words in the verse which says, 'And I will show him [Paul] how much he must suffer for Me' (TLB), are true for me? What if God has, for this time, actually *called* me to suffer? What if I have thirty or thirty-five more years to live here on earth and there will be no healing, only the call to suffer?"

We were stopped now, standing facing each other on the sidewalk; and I shall never, ever, forget Chuck's words. This learned man; this seminary graduate; this godly, teachable man; this beautifully wise man answered all my questions with an honest, "I don't know."

It was an *incredible* moment for me, and a real inner healing began to take place. Then, as we continued walking, Chuck spoke what I really believe were words of truth from the Source of all Truth, our Lord. He talked of one of life's greatest mysteries, the fact that there *were* some things in life which could not be explained. There were, he said, some questions in life which simply could *not be answered.* And there were some circumstances, trials, and testings, which could *never* be understood.

In those healing moments, I began to grasp in my heart that it was absolutely all right if some things were beyond our sphere of understanding. It's all right to honestly admit, "I don't know," even if you are a pastor, a church leader, or layperson. I began to feel a deep sense of relief, and I reasoned, "Okay, maybe when we get to heaven we'll ask God the whys of our pain and suffering. Maybe He'll have all the answers we think we need to hear. Maybe He won't answer at all. But, either way, for *now* I'll accept the truth that there are some things which defy all explanations." I accepted the premise that only God really knows those kinds of answers. And I decided to trust those iron-weighted questions into His safekeeping.

Before Chuck left that night, he talked briefly with my family and me. He explained to them that I had no hope whatsoever and then proceeded to say, "Nobody is stating the obvious here, so I will. I think God is changing your message, Joyce. And one of these days you are going to write a book on pain that will relate to everyone who has ever suffered."

I remember smiling in disbelief and saying, "Chuck, I love your confidence in my writing abilities, but how can I write about the subject of pain when I have absolutely no answers for it?"

He shrugged his shoulders and just assured me that I would indeed write a book for people in pain, especially people who don't hear the music anymore.

It was a strange sensation. There I was, wanting desperately to leave this world, to be done with the work here and go home to heaven, while at the same time Chuck was opening the creative track in my brain about writing another book.

Chuck stood between us and prayed in the driveway just before he left. Yet even during his beautiful prayer I wondered how I'd live even one more day with this pain, much less live long enough to write about it. And what of hope? How do you live without hope? ♥

*". . . It is not to the credit of*
*my faith for healing that I am*
*more well today. Just, slowly,*
*God did what He had planned—*
*uniquely for me.*

*". . . If I had been healed, I wouldn't*
*have suffered, and I would have missed*
*the extra love God passed out."*

—Excerpts from a
friend's letter

♥

The day after I talked with Chuck Swindoll, I flew to Fort Wayne, Indiana, to speak at the Bible college located there. The people were wonderful, and the Lord mercifully helped me to overcome the pain long enough to speak; but, I came home late Sunday evening sick, discouraged, depressed, and completely exhausted.

A few mornings later my phone rang. The caller was my long-term friend, Dr. Keith Korstjens (author of *Not a Sometimes Love*). He'd been up most of the night, praying about me and searching the Scriptures for just the right thing to say to me. He'd poured out his heart to God, about me and my pain. Now he wanted to talk.

I was at a place in life—racked with constant pain and the natural by-product of illness, depression—when I seemed to be quite allergic to people and their letters which evaluated that pain and depression. Most Christians can't spell *depression* much less admit they have it. So if you're brave enough to talk about it, you take on a whole boatload of criticism. And even when I've been well, I've never reacted too graciously when given unsolicited advice. (Have you?) But at that moment, the Lord raised a little flag in the back of my mind and whispered, "Listen up. This is important!" So I reasoned: If the Lord had just prepared me to hear, then possibly He had prepared Keith to speak. Besides, if an old and trusted friend (a pastor yet!) has spent the preceding night in prayer on my behalf, then he had certainly earned the right to say to me just about anything he wanted to say.

"Talk to me," I said.

Keith explained that he was deeply concerned about the volume of mail I was getting from people who held the concept that "You are not healed because you *don't* have faith or you *do* have sin." He'd searched the Scriptures he said, and each time he had come back to the story of the paralytic man. The man had been healed, but it had not been his own faith which beautifully compelled Jesus to heal him. Oh, it had been *faith,* all right; but it was the faith of the man's four friends—*not* his own.

In three places (Matthew 9, Mark 2, and Luke 5), the Scriptures tell us clearly that Jesus, *seeing* the faith of the paralytic's friends, healed the man.

With a new awareness, even as Keith talked, I recalled another prime example of a man whose faith was not responsible for his healing—yet an incredible healing had taken place in his life. This was undeniably true in the case of Lazarus. The brother of Mary and Martha had been *dead* for four days when Jesus gave him the ultimate of all healings! His faith, or lack of it, had nothing to do with God's healing. But the healing had everything to do with God's sovereign plan.

What I treasured the most about Keith's phone call, besides the love that prompted it, was the practical application of his theology which, as nearly as I can recollect, went like this: "Joyce, the paralytic man had no faith of his own, but his *friends* did. I am your friend. So I asked God what, as that friend, I could *do* for you in regard to faith. The Lord so explicitly said, '*Loan her your faith.*' So I've called to tell you that I've got lots of faith. I'm not low on it at all, and I'm joyfully loaning you all the faith you need . . . for as long as you need it. And when someone accuses you of being sub-spiritual because you appear to have no faith, you just tell them that you've got plenty now."

I was so jazzed about Keith's loaning me his faith that I called Chuck Swindoll to tell him.

"Isn't that incredible, Chuck? Just when the mail is mounting about my having no faith, Keith loans me his—interest free, for as long as I need it!"

"I'll tell you what I'll do," Chuck boomed enthusiastically back. "Since you don't have any hope, I'll *loan* you mine! I've got all the hope in the world for you, Joyce! And I'll go you even one better . . . I'm going to ask *Jesus* to loan you His love."

Emil Brunner once said, "What oxygen is to the lungs, such is hope for the meaning of life."

I am convinced we do not spend our life in the pursuit of happiness or in the quest for instant rewards, but rather in the pursuit of purpose in life. We want to live meaningful lives. Hope is the magic ingredient that fuels our energies to vigorously pursue a meaningful life and gives us the power to carry out our mission to accomplishment. Without hope we are without the oxygen to go on.

Chuck was loaning me *his* hope and *Jesus'* love. Perhaps that was just the oxygen I needed to go on breathing.

I put down the phone and sat at my desk for a long time savoring Keith's and Chuck's conversations. Then I replayed the concept of both "loans" on my mind. An enormous amount of ground had been covered, yet somehow I began to sense that there was a small puzzle piece still missing.

I went over the loan applications again. I could understand how Keith, loaded with glowing faith, could loan me his; and I could understand exactly how Chuck could loan me his heart full of hope . . . but what gnawed at me was the part about Jesus loaning me His love. How would that work out? I mean, in practical, seeable, feelable ways how does Jesus loan *anybody* His love?

A letter from Keith came as a follow-up to our conversation, and it was very helpful. (Remember, when people are in great pain, they have a hard time hearing past their suffering. They may need written words, or just a tiny card, to penetrate their suffering.) But, it was a letter, dated September 15, from Keith's wife, Mary, that provided the piece to the puzzle of my understanding.

Her letter, painstakingly handwritten (Mary was paralyzed by polio over twenty-five years ago and has very limited use of her hands), was a genuine clue in the "hows" of Jesus loaning His love. Mary wrote:

Dear Joyce,

How we love you! How our hearts ache for you and with you.

Please forgive us for not keeping aware of how you are doing. The last we had heard, there was *some* relief from pain. Will you forgive our/my neglect?

I wish I had explanations and/or magical powers . . . or? Or whatever.

I wait with you,
I ask *why* with you,
I ask *how long* for you.
I hold you in love and
I cry for you!

If knowing you are loved, cared about, prayed for and wept over, helps at all . . . that is what Keith and I offer.

In deepest love,
Mary and Keith

Ah ha! Mary's letter illuminated my thinking as though she had turned on a battery of lights in a very dark auditorium. I could see it so clearly, yet it was so simple—it was almost ridiculous.

*Jesus loans us His love through the faces, hearts, touches, and responses of His children!* Keith's, Mary's, and Chuck's expressions of caring concern were so genuine and so unconditional, the only thing I could see was God's reflected, *loaned* love.

I began to rethink all the times I had seen or heard the Lord in one of His children. Easily I could see the dear faces of family and friends close to me, and I knew instantly that the looks in their eyes and the beauty of their faces were the looks and the beauty of Jesus. He was *in them,* loaning me His sustaining love.

Years ago I had written the lyrics and music to several songs. (I wrote my first piece, "The Jungle Song," after my second or third piano lesson when I was just a little girl.) But with the painful jaw spasms of temporomandibular joint stress dysfunction which started in 1973 and the increasing head pain, I found that singing, playing the piano, or concentrating long enough to compose music just ceased to happen. Yet, around the twentieth of September, I sat down at the piano and wrote my first song in more than nine years. The chorus came first, because that's the essence of what I was feeling, and then the verses. ♥

## YOUR DEAR FACE

*Hold me up, I cannot stand;*
*Wrap your love around my soul.*
*I've no faith, so loan me yours;*
*I think I've lost my hold.*

*Joy and hope have ebbed away;*
*I cannot face tomorrow, much less today.*
*Hug me with your words; put your arms under mine;*
*Hold me up until I'm fine.*

*Gather 'round and hold us up,*
*We who drink this bitter cup.*
*Our strength is gone, our hearts despair;*
*By God's love, show us that you care.*

Chorus:

*For if I'm to see*
*Anything of God's mercy and grace,*
*Let me see it, O child of God,*
*On your dear face.*

*Your dear face, your dear face,*
*You are so special to me;*
*For in your dear face, yes, your dear face,*
*It is Jesus, caring Jesus, that I see.*

—Joyce Landorf

♥

It dawned on me, slowly at first and then with more speed and clarity, that if I couldn't hear the music or the voice of God in this, the most silent of all my Septembers, then I would listen and look to the voices and the faces of others. To my surprise and joy, I began to see the Lord. There were moments of His mercy and glimpses of His grace even though He was still silent and I was still broken and unhealed.

On the twenty-fifth day of that silent September, I was scheduled to speak at two of the morning services in the large Wesleyan church, called Skyline, in the San Diego area of Southern California. I'd spoken there several times in years past, but always for mother and daughter banquets. I had never met Skyline's new pastor, Dr. John Maxwell.

Skyline had just shown my film series, *His Stubborn Love,* and Pastor Maxwell was enthusiastic about my being there for the Sunday services.

Eagerly we drove down to San Diego early that weekend and

stayed with our friends, the Bamesbergers, but I was not much fun to be around because the pain came on and locked into level three. It completely destroyed my joy and my enthusiasm for speaking.

I came close to cancelling the engagement because I was so deathly ill, but I could feel the Holy Spirit's gentle pushing in my heart. And by Sunday morning there was a strong sense of urgency within me. I knew it was best to stay, to speak, and to meet this pastor and his people.

Had I not gone that Sunday, I would have missed one of the most healing experiences of my life.

I was stunned by the overwhelming, loving warmth of every person I met:

- The pastor.
- His staff.
- The men who prayed with us before the service.
- The continual references to my being there.
- The uplifting prayers prayed *during* the service *before* I spoke.
- The faces of the people. (Oh, the faces . . . those precious faces!)

In all my nearly twenty years of speaking, I had never before experienced such an outpouring of God Himself.

The church seats one thousand, and each service was packed with people. I felt such oneness with them. Briefly during the first service, the choir's music, mingled with the presence of

God, was so overpowering that I had to leave the platform, go out, cry, and repair my mascara. When I finally did speak, I told the congregation some of the incidents which marked my fierce struggle with continuous pain, and I asked them to be my "Balcony People" and my encouragers. It was one of those times when I know I said what I felt God would have me say; but, it was the pastors, musicians, and congregation who did the *ministering* that morning.

I ended each service by singing publicly for the first time my song, "Your Dear Face." Their response was unreal!

Not one single person told me why I was unhealed and still broken. No one rejected me because I was depressed or because I wanted to go home to be with the Lord. No one suggested that I had a serious lack of faith or that some sin in my life was blocking the healing hand of God. No one, of the hundreds that came up to me after each service, gave me smug, surface comments like "The answer to your pain is Jesus." And no one politely patted me on the back with a trite "God bless."

Instead, they held me, wept with me, gently touched my face, and pledged their love and prayer support. We became each other's "Balcony Person." I was overwhelmed by Jesus' love, so radiant in those wonderful people.

Before I left that Sunday, John Maxwell told me that he had a men's prayer group which met every month. He explained that each year the men take on two outside-the-church prayer projects—one usually a missionary request, the other local. He said that the men wanted to know if I'd be willing to let them take me on as one of those special projects. They would be praying separately each day and together with the pastors on a monthly basis. They wanted to pray for my health, my marriage, and my calling.

Was I willing¿ I couldn't say yes fast enough! A men's prayer group praying for me¿ A woman¿ It was an astounding, gorgeous thing, and I could hardly believe it.

I have a marvelous group of women in Pomona, California, who have prayed regularly for me now for about ten years. And many women in churches all over hold me up in their prayer groups and in church prayer chains. But no church I'd ever been in, anywhere in the world, had made such an offer involving the leadership of the church and the *men* of the congregation.

The Skyline men's prayer group, headed by Pastor Maxwell, is now in their second year of praying regularly for me. They, along with many women's groups, have made a world of difference in my life.

Christ's love which shines from a congregation of people like this—people who are dedicated to a prayer ministry for one another—is so bright it's almost blinding. It's Jesus *loaning* His love in action . . . not just in principle.

The following Thursday morning, I came home from teaching my Bible study class at Betty Manning's to find Janet Keough (the leader of my Pomona prayer group) and Sheila Rapp (my secretary and a member of the prayer group) standing in my driveway.

It was wonderful to see them. But since they are both very active homemakers and it was a long drive from their homes to mine, I asked, "What in the world are you doing here¿" They just asked *me* where my freezer was and took an enormous ice chest out of the trunk of Janet's car.

Well, I'm a bit sensitive about my refrigerator or my freezer! It's an old habit. Actually, I didn't want anyone to poke around in the freezer because I knew it contained two packages of hot dog buns, one very old freezer-burned pound of hamburger, and an enormous ice build-up. (I hadn't defrosted it for at least four years. Still haven't, either.)

Long after Janet and Sheila left, I crept out to the garage to stare inside my freezer. It was transformed. They had filled it full of delicious goodies. It was bulging with care-packages.

The women of my Pomona prayer group had prepared, wrapped, and sent all kinds of foodstuffs. There were chicken and meat casseroles, homemade soups, chili; and even jams, dozens of bran muffins, corn bread, fancy breads, brownies, and cakes. I was stunned by all the time, effort, and thought that had gone into that display of love.

Everything was packed in a disposable dish, jar, or pan, so I wouldn't have to return anything to the giver. But, I couldn't have returned any pan or dish to the giver anyway, because there were no identifying names. It was very surprising—especially in this age of most everyone wanting credit or recognition for things they've done—yet there was no clue, other than it was from the prayer group, as to who made what! Nobody's *name* was on anything. They had tagged each item as to what it was, and there were directions for heating if necessary, but that was all. The only thing I was told was that it was food to be used on a day when I was too sick to plan or cook meals.

Janet and Sheila also brought another big box. It contained many gift-wrapped, handmade items, and there was also a big stack of cards and letters. Again, nothing identified the sender, and the instructions were the same. I was to open one package/letter a day on the "baddest" of days.

When I asked Sheila why they had gone to all this work, she had anwered, "I've been waiting a long time to do this for you . . . like you did for me. Don't you remember?" No, I didn't.

She reminded me of the time she'd been burned on her hands and stomach in an accident with cooking oil that had caught fire. When I had visited her in the hospital, I always came with little gifts, cards, letters, and especially newspaper cartoons. Then for a month, after she came home, I left unmarked packages of food, plants, and little gifts on her doorstep. I'd ring the bell, run, and never admit my involvement. It was something that had happened years ago, and while I remembered the accident, I had forgotten the little things I had done at the time. But dear Sheila . . . she'd waited to do something special for me as I had for her. Sheila's timing was magnificent.

I wonder, does anything happen to God's people by chance or coincidence? I doubt it. Those precious women of my prayer group, by their tangible gifts, were loaning me Jesus' love in one of the most down-to-earth ways possible. In my mind's eye, I can still see the inside of our freezer, crammed with all kinds of delicious things. But I believe the freezer contained more than food, for it held also the love of God, borne out of a practical theology.

If I am to be honest, however, then I must also tell you that none of the special gifts loaned to me (faith, hope, and love) took the pain away. Those offerings of love, as beautiful as they were, didn't even lift the edge off of my daily suffering. Slowly, somewhere in the closed, shut-down parts of my heart and mind, I began to realize I could hear the faint strains of music. It was only an echo-type sound, and I was still just as sick as before, but I suspected that there was music out there and that it *might* get louder and more discernible.

Gradually, Keith's "loaned" faith, Chuck's hope, and the Jesus-love from family and friends began to sift and filter through the layers of my pain and brokenness. I began to think that maybe, just maybe, there *might* be a meaning and a purpose in all this pain. ♥

Your dear face, your dear face,
You are so special to me;
For in your dear face, yes, your dear face,
It is Jesus, caring Jesus, that I see.

Trust in those *who have hope for you when it's almost impossible for you to hope for yourself.*

Trust in yourself *when your best instincts tell you that hope is more in perseverance than in active or passive self-destruction.*

Trust in God, *silent and absent as He may appear. He must* be . . . *and being, He must care and be in the pursuit of solutions not readily apparent.*

Trust! *Though you give up all else . . . never give up trusting . . . even when you doubt . . . and hurt.*

—Francis Heatherley
September 1982

♥

In the opening pages of this book, I copied from my pain journal these words,

> Yet here, in my heart, I cannot see, hear, touch, or feel God; and the silence of my life is deadly. God seems to be doing nothing— nothing at all.

That statement alone tells you that my God-concept was pretty distorted, or possibly nonexistent. Pain changes our perspective on everything . . . especially our thoughts about God. I really believe, with all my heart, that many suffering children of God see our heavenly Father through those same pain-warped lenses. But, I also believe that the years of suffering in our lives *can be* beautifully used to peel back the thick layers of pretense and hypocrisy. Unvarnished suffering can allow us to establish a clear, unmarred picture of the true identity and integrity of God.

I had to reexamine my God-concept. For I had come to realize that often we base our concept of God on someone else's experience or someone else's belief and not our own.

One God-concept in current vogue has reached epidemic levels of popularity. For lack of a better term, I call it *fad theology*.

It's quite popular now, in the mid-eighties, for Christians to say they absolutely *know* what God thinks. They assert that if they *claim* a verse of Scripture, God must do what *they* ask. They pinpoint the reasons for our being unhealed as a lack of faith or the presence of sin. This view of Scripture compels our minds to run in very narrow grooves, further damaging our God-concept. And, instead of bringing the healing of the Holy Spirit to our souls, it leaves us even more wounded than before; and we are breathless with our efforts to transverse the steep sides of a new mountain called guilt.

So what of us who love the Lord, whose sins have been forgiven and whose faith, although shaken, is still intact? The fad theology of today does not address our problem; for we still blindly trust, we still continue to endure and persevere, and we still love our sovereign God. What of us? Is it really true we would be healed if we stopped sinning and conjured up some more faith? Is it that simple? I doubt it.

Take, for example, Joni Eareckson Tada. What if her church had banded together in the weeks after her accident and really prayed for her healing, and God had miraculously, instantly healed her? How long do you think the body of Christ would have rejoiced over her healing or remembered her? (I figure about thirty seconds at the least and three weeks at the most.)

Instead, God chose to use her unhealed state and consequently gave her a world-wide ministry. Had she been healed, it is quite possible we may have never seen her artwork, heard her sparkling testimony, read her books, or listened to her singing albums. Today her life from a wheelchair sheds a bright light on God's marvelous plans and sovereignty. *But she remains unhealed.*

Recently, when I was on a speaking engagement, an anonymous message was slipped into my papers. It said:

> When you spoke of receiving letters telling you that, since you'd suffered nine years, there must still be sin in your life or you must have too little faith, it occurred to me that we can't *bribe* God by being less sinful or more faithful.
>
> Whatever you do or don't do, have or don't have, God will continue to love you.

Oh, how I needed to be reminded of God's unconditional love toward all of His children. It helps to offset the drumbeat of the fad theologians' message that "Jesus wants everybody well . . . and, if you're not healthy, wealthy, and wise, it's not God's fault but yours."

How can this pop God-concept be preached by sincere brothers and sisters in Christ while at the same time they ignore passage after passage of Scripture which deals with God's people and the stark reality of life as it truly is? How can these fad theologians read the Bible and fail to see that biblical characters constantly endeavored to cope with suffering, pain, death, and trials of every shape and size?

Are we, as God's present-day people, any different? Are we, unlike Job or Paul, exempt from hurting? Has God changed the nature of evil in our present world so we *always escape suffering?* Or, is this deliberate and widespread emphasis on living on a continuous spiritual high—experiencing a miracle a minute and being caught up in prosperity principles—*denying* the reality of God's Word? I think this cover-up of what the Bible teaches beats the government's Watergate cover-up by a country mile.

The doctrine of suffering fills an enormous number of pages in the Bible. To deny this fact is to turn our magnificent, multi-faceted, megaton-powerful God into a flat, one-dimensional, plastic credit card to be used at our whim and discretion.

If we are to buy the "claim it and it's yours" theory, then we'll have to delete all the references David made in Psalms—which span much of his entire life—when he acknowledged again and again that he was in deep agony, far from being well and whole. What's more, God *could have* obliterated all references to suffering in the Scriptures. But, like sin and its consequences, suffering is a part of living; and, amazingly enough, God dealt with both sin and suffering with no attempt to cover up either one.

When you and I are in the middle of an illness, a crisis, a divorce, or bereavement and some profound suffering consumes our entire life, we must steadfastly search for the true image of God. We cannot accept someone else's God-concept.

During my search for a balanced, believable, and true God in my agony, God Himself was very faithful to me. He made good His promise found in Deuteronomy 4:29–31.

But you will also begin to search again for Jehovah your God, and you shall find him when you search for him with all your hearts and souls. When those bitter days have come upon you in the latter times, you will finally return to the Lord your God and listen to what he tells you. For the Lord your God is merciful—he will not abandon you nor destroy you nor forget the promises he has made to your ancestors (TLB).

I did not have to *claim* these verses as God's ironclad promises to me. I just threw myself on God's mercy, searched for Him with all my heart and soul and—true to His Word—*He let me find Him.*

Tremendous insight and changes in my God-concept were brought about by a number of things, but none so powerful as ten pages on pain and God from a friend.

On October 13, 1982, Francis Heatherley (or "Doc," as he is known to many), handed me his handwritten pages entitled "On Pain, God, You, and Those of Us Who Love You."

I took the folder of pages with me that day to the Azusa Pacific University library where I was doing my initial research on biblical women for *He Began with Eve.* I'll never forget the experience of reading those ten pages.

God's presence, strong like a magnificent perfume, began to fill the room. I would read one paragraph, stop, inhale the fragrance, and then wordlessly tell God how wonderful it was to feel His presence again. I could hear His voice, I could see His face, and I could feel His arms about me in the pages I was reading. The tears of joy would not stop flowing.

Part of Francis's writings reminded me that God is in a spiritual war. The battle between good and evil goes on. We know that ultimately God will win. We know we are on the winning side. But in the meantime it's difficult, if not downright impossible, to endure. One of the most touching paragraphs was this one:

> Would a God of love either perpetrate this pain or permit it, if He could do otherwise right now? I think not. I think rather He is the primary head of the universe, who is triumphing over the unholy powers of His multiple kingdom, who has *not yet* put all His enemies down to defeat. But who will *ultimately* prevail.

In light of Doc's statement, I couldn't help remembering a line from Margaret Clarkson's book, *Destined for Glory,* which said, "Though the decisive battle [at Calvary] has been won, the war is not over yet." I needed to be reminded of the war and of the ultimate victor.

On yet another page in Doc's letter, he posed this question:

> With all the good God has done for us . . . with all the grace He has shown . . . with His continuing determination to right the wrongs . . . with His long history of overcoming evil with good . . . can we not now say, even in our pain, "Lord, I am with You. I know You would heal me now if You could. I know my pain is utterly frustrating to You. You have been so good to me in every way You could, I will not desert You now. In spite of my suffering I am on Your side. I respond to Your love, regardless of Your present limitations and the battles You are waging."

Joyce, can we not say these things to our God?

I was euphoric as I read my friend's words, and I found myself soaring on the wings of hope and joy. I could hear the music of God again, and this time the music was loud and that of a full symphony orchestra. It seemed that the voices of countless saints of God—those gone on before and those present-day brothers and sisters in Christ—were singing the great song of God . . . *just for me*. It was a rare and moving moment of my life.

Being in level three pain at the time of that reading, I was really comforted beyond measure by another paragraph which stated this beautiful prayer:

> You know, Lord, I am hurting immeasurably; and there will be times when this pain blinds me to Your love and power. But I will recover from these blind spots, time and time again, and rally to the support of Your loving cause. Thank You, Lord, for being my devoted, caring, frustrated heavenly Father, even when my sight is dimmed by my tortured body.

Not many people had allowed me to say openly that I did not "see or feel" God. No one had given me the permission I needed to be honest about my blind spots. And no one, except this dear friend, saw *beyond* my blindness to remind me it was only temporary and that I'd rally again and again!

What hope those ten pages poured into my spirit! It was as though Francis Heatherley had pulled back the heavy curtains of my pain to reveal the true and precious God I had searched for and longed to see. I found myself face to face with the awesome God of my salvation, and I fell deeply in love with this precious God.

I saw the Lord sitting beside me on my bed of pain—much like a parent who has done everything for His very sick child, and who now just quietly waits out the night. I envisioned God holding my face in His hands. I could see the tears streaming down His face, and I could hear Him say, "Joyce, my child, ultimately I will triumph. Ultimately, I will bring meaning out of all of this suffering. Ultimately, I will overcome Satan and eradicate the sin and evil which abounds in this world. Ultimately, I *shall* make you completely whole. I will pour the balm of Gilead over your life and you will suffer no more."

And, because Francis knows something of the immense struggle for those of us in pain to go on enduring until God's "ultimate" is accomplished, he wrote:

> I cannot fault you if you are not always able to acclaim God's hope in the midst of your pain . . . and I don't believe God faults you. I believe rather that He loves you, sheds His own tears for you, and relishes the day when His wise, powerful, and loving process will win over the forces of evil and bring comfort and ease for you . . . and millions like you throughout the universe.
>
> Though I feel with you intensely, I cannot possibly know the full suffering of your endurance, but I urge you to persevere in your trust and love for the God who is tortured by your pain and who will *ultimately* overcome . . . perhaps even in the days at hand.

To those of you still hurting and still in your own painful silent September, I pray:

- *May others around you (even me) loan you their faith, their hope, and Jesus' love.*

- *May the Lord cover your ears, so the thoughtless and critical remarks about your suffering go unheard.*

- *May you not lose heart because of the attacks from Satan (and some of God's children).*

- *May God's children give you the freedom to say what you are honestly feeling without being judgmental or critical of your spirit.*

- *May you not grow weary of well-doing and sharing as you wait on God's timing.*

- *May you hear the music of God loudly and clearly in spite of the thunderous noise of pain.*

- *May you continue to endure and trust even when you are past enduring and trusting because you know the Holy Spirit intercedes on your behalf.*

- *And, lastly, may you understand that the silence of this agonizing September will not last forever. Someday, somehow, and sometime God will ultimately rescue you and you shall emerge from the war triumphant and whole!* ♥

*"And the Lord will continually guide you,*
*And satisfy your desire in scorched places,*
*And give strength to your bones;*
*And you will be like a watered garden,*
*And like a spring of water whose waters*
*    do not fail."*

—Isaiah 58:11 (NASB)

♥

Just a few months ago, although there had been little or no change in the daily patterns of my pain, my daughter Laurie sensed the working of God in my life . . . and in hers. She wrote in a letter:

Mom, I have given so much thought to your pain. Whatever happens about it, whatever you do about it—I will always love you. And even if you die, I will miss you terribly . . . but I am beginning to see beyond the pain, and see into your heart.

I want the pain to end for you . . . it's just so hard to understand. Pain and suffering is absolutely the *pits* with no sweetness of the cherries.

Thank you for your love. But, most of all, thank you for staying one more day.

Always,
Laurie

Her last line, "Thank you for staying one more day," is exactly what I want to leave with you.

I love you, dear unseen fellow sufferer, and from the depths of my heart *I thank you for staying one more day*. And though painful it must be, I ask you, "Please stay one more day."

I encourage you to listen for the sounds of God's music, for we shall hear it and *we shall be made whole*. Whether the music of our healing comes tomorrow, two weeks from now, years from now, or only in death when we see Him face to face, *ultimately* we shall be rescued, and we shall suffer no more. ♥

## ABOUT THE AUTHOR

Joyce Landorf Heatherley is known nationwide as a uniquely gifted Christian communicator, able to convey Biblical principles with relevance, humor, compassion and gentle conviction—in a way that speaks to the needs of men and women from all backgrounds. A best-selling author of both fiction and non-fiction (her 21 books include *BALCONY PEOPLE, SILENT SEPTEMBER, IRREGULAR PEOPLE, HE BEGAN WITH EVE, CHANGE-POINTS, UNWORLD PEOPLE, MOURNING SONG, JOSEPH,* and *I CAME TO LOVE YOU LATE* (with her 22nd book, *THE INHERITANCE,* due for publication in Fall, 1989), she is also an immensely popular speaker and conference leader. Recordings of her more popular talks, including *BALCONY PEOPLE, IRREGULAR PEOPLE, UN-WORLD PEOPLE* and *THE INHERITANCE* are available on audio cassette, as are video tapes of *CHANGEPOINTS, IRREGULAR PEOPLE,* and *UNWORLD PEOPLE.* Her *HIS STUBBORN LOVE* film series, based on her nationally acclaimed seminars of the same name, was the recipient of the 1981 President's Award from the Christian Film Distributors Association.

Any speaking engagement requests or inquiries concerning Joyce Landorf Heatherley books, tapes, and films may be directed to:

Balcony Publishing, Inc.
3011 Highway 620 North
Austin, Texas 78734